How To Bake And Ice Petit Fours

By
Brenda Van Niekerk

Second Edition 2018

ISBN-13:978-1502862853
ISBN-10:1502862859

Contents

Petit Fours

A petit four is a small confectionery generally served as part of dessert or eaten with coffee.

There are 2 different categories of Petits Fours:

1) Petits fours secs – sec meaning "dry".

2) Petits fours glacés - glacé meaning "iced".

Macarons

Dainty
Biscuits

Puff
pastries

4

Petits Fours Secs

This group includes a variety of small desserts such as:

- Special dainty biscuits

- Baked meringues

- Macarons

- Puff pastries

Baked Meringues

Small
éclairs

Tartlets

Petits Fours Glacés

Petits fours glacés are iced or decorated in some way. The miniature cakes are covered in fondant or glacé icing and decorated beautifully with fondant flowers and piping. Each of these cakes is a miniature art piece.

This group includes:

- Small éclairs

- Tartlets

- Fondant covered cakes

Fondant covered cakes

Classical Petit Fours Glacés

Recipe

Ingredients For Sponge Cake

8 eggs

1 egg yolk

125 ground almonds

Zest from 1 lemon

180 g sugar

180 g flour

Ingredients For Filling

180 g smooth apricot jam

250 g marzipan

1 egg white

Ingredients For Boiled icing

100 g margarine

280 g icing sugar

25 ml milk

Ingredients For Butterscotch Icing

30 g butter

30 ml brown sugar

30 ml evaporated milk

Method To Bake The Cake

Beat the egg yolks, ground almonds, lemon zest and ½ the sugar until thick and creamy.

Whisk the egg whites until stiff peaks form.

Fold the remaining sugar into the egg whites and beat until stiff.

Fold the egg yolks into the egg whites.

Fold in the flour.

Combine well.

Pour the mixture into a greased baking pan and smooth evenly on the top.

Bake at 220 degrees C for 12 minutes.

Remove the cake from the pan and cool the cake on a wire rack.

Cut the cake horizontally into 2 halves.

Spread the bottom layer of cake with the apricot jam.

Place the other layer of cake on top of the jam layer.

Press down well.

Wrap the cake in foil and place a heavy wooden board on top of the cake.

Leave the cake for 24 hours.

Method To Cover The Cake With Marzipan

Cut the cake into various miniature shapes.

Brush the cake with the egg white.

Cover each piece of cake with marzipan.

Mold the shape carefully with the marzipan.

Leave the marzipan to dry.

Method To Make The Boiled Icing

Melt the margarine.

Heat the milk.

Combine the melted margarine, heated milk and ½ the icing sugar together in a saucepan.

Bring the mixture to the boil without stirring.

Remove from heat as soon as boiling point is reached.

Stir in remaining icing sugar. Blend well.

Work quickly as the icing hardens.

Add the flavoring and coloring as desired (see section on Color The Boiled Icing and Flavor The Boiled Icing).

Pour the icing over the cakes.

Smooth with a wet palette knife.

Leave to set.

Method To Make The Butterscotch Icing

Combine the butter, brown sugar and evaporated milk together in a saucepan.

Heat the mixture until the sugar has melted.

Bring to boil and stop stirring.

Boil for 10 to 15 minutes until the mixture has thickened.

Pour the icing over the cakes.

Smooth with a wet palette knife.

Leave to set.

Color The Boiled Icing

There Are 3 Types Of Food Coloring:

- Gel

- Powder

- Paste

The gel food coloring is more concentrated than the liquid food coloring.

Using gel food coloring will not thin down the chocolate like the liquid food coloring will do.

How To Make Different Colors

Using the 3 primary colors – red, blue and yellow you can mix any other color that you need.

To Make Orange

Mix equal parts red and yellow

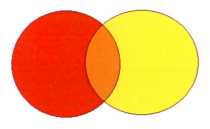

To Make Purple

Mix equal parts red and blue.

To Make Black

Mix 3 parts red, 3 parts blue, and 2 parts green.

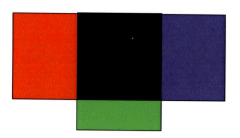

Color Wheel

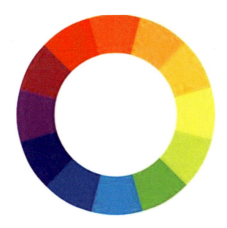

Flavor The Boiled Icing

There are many options which you can use to flavor your boiled icing:

- Any type of extract – vanilla, lemon, orange and rose water are but a few that come to mind.

- You can also add lemon or orange zest for additional zing to your icing.

- You could use any liqueurs to flavor the icing.

Decorating The Petit Fours

Petit Fours are always beautifully decorated.

Ways To Decorate Petit Fours:

- Candied edible flowers

- Plastic white and dark chocolate flowers and decorations

- Fondant modelled flowers and decorations

- Glace cherries

- Chopped assorted nuts

- Edible cake glitter

- Ready bought edible cake decorations

- Chocolate curls and leaves

- Piped icing or chocolate

A La Ritz Petit Fours

Ingredients For The Pastry

190 g flour

65 g castor sugar

1 egg

25 ml water

95 g butter

Ingredients For The Filling

4 egg yolks

125 g castor sugar

4 ml salt

15 g corn flour

250 ml milk

1 ml vanilla extract

200 g butter

80 g icing sugar

12,5 ml cocoa powder

12,5 ml boiling water

To Assemble A La Ritz Petit Fours

Chopped nuts

Red glace cherries

Green glace cherries

Method To Make the Pastry

Sift the flour.

Add the sugar, egg, water and butter.

Mix well.

Wrap pastry in plastic and refrigerate for 2 hours.

Roll the pastry out to a 3mm thickness.

Cut out rounds using a 4cm cookie cutter.

Place the rounds on a greased baking sheet.

Bake at 200 degrees C for 8 to 10 minutes.

Remove from the baking pan and cool the pastry shells on a baking rack.

Method To Make The Filling

Combine the egg yolks, sugar, salt, corn flour and a little of the milk together.

Heat the remaining milk and vanilla extract in a saucepan.

Stir in the corn flour mixture.

Bring to the boil, stirring all the while.

Cook for 10 minutes until the mixture has thickened, stir constantly.

Allow the mixture to cool.

Stir frequently.

Cream the icing sugar and butter together until light and creamy.

Slowly combine the icing sugar mixture and custard mixture together.

Beat very well.

Divide the mixture into 2.

Mix the cocoa powder and boiling water together.

Combine the cocoa powder paste with the one half of the filling.

Mix well.

Place both lots of filling in separate piping bags with rosette nozzles.

Pipe the chocolate filling onto half the pastry shells and the plain filling onto the other half.

Decorate with red and green glace cherries and chopped nuts.

Éclair Recipes

Chocolate Éclairs

Ingredients

250 ml water

125 ml margarine

250 ml flour

3 eggs

125 ml cream

12,5 ml castor sugar

Chocolate (melted)

Method

Melt the margarine and water together in a saucepan.

Add the flour all at once.

Beat thoroughly.

Allow the mixture to cool.

Beat in 1 egg at a time.

Blend well.

Place the mixture in a piping bag with a large star nozzle.

Pipe the éclairs onto a greased baking sheet.

Bake at 190 degrees C for 20 minutes.

Lower the temperature to 160 degrees C.

Bake for a further 15 minutes.

Split the éclairs along the length and allow the éclairs to cool on a wire rack.

Whip the cream and the sugar together until stiff peaks are formed.

Place the whipped cream into a piping bag with a nozzle and pipe the cream into the éclairs when the éclairs are cold.

Drizzle the melted chocolate over the top of the éclairs.

Custard Choux Buns

Ingredients

250 ml water

125 ml margarine

250 ml flour

3 eggs

Ingredients For Custard Filling

250 ml cream (beaten stiff)

200 ml cold milk

1 instant vanilla pudding mix

Icing sugar to sprinkle over choux buns

Method

Melt the margarine and water together in a saucepan.

Add the flour all at once.

Beat thoroughly.

Allow the mixture to cool.

Beat in 1 egg at a time.

Blend well.

Place the mixture in a piping bag with a large star nozzle.

Pipe the rosettes onto a greased baking sheet.

Bake at 190 degrees C for 20 minutes.

Lower the temperature to 160 degrees C.

Bake for a further 15 minutes.

Split the choux buns along the length and allow the choux buns to cool on a wire rack.

Combine the milk and instant vanilla pudding together.

Blend well.

Fold in the cream.

Refrigerate the custard filling for 5 minutes.

Place the custard filling into a piping bag with a nozzle and pipe the custard filling into the choux buns when the choux buns are cold.

Sprinkle the icing sugar over the choux buns.

Tartlet Recipes

Fruit Custard Tartlets

Ingredients For The Pastry

180 g flour

4 ml salt

125 g butter

20 g castor sugar

1 egg yolk

10 ml iced water

Castor sugar to sprinkle on pastry shells

Ingredients For The Filling

30 g butter

30 g flour

12,5 ml castor sugar

1 egg yolk

150 ml milk

1 ml vanilla extract

Ingredients For Fruit Filling

Selection of canned fruit

Ingredients For The Glaze

75 ml apricot jam (heated)

Method For Making The Pastry Shells

Combine the flour and salt together.

Rub in the butter until the mixture resembles breadcrumbs.

Add the sugar.

Mix well.

Combine the egg yolk and water together.

Combine the flour mixture and egg mixture together.

Knead well on a floured surface.

Roll the pastry out to a 6mm thickness.

Cut out rounds with a cookie cutter.

Place the circles in greased patty pans.

Prick the pastry rounds with a fork.

Refrigerate the pans for 30 minutes.

Bake at 190 degrees C for 20 minutes.

Remove from the oven.

Sprinkle with the pastry shells with castor sugar while they are still hot.

Method For Making The Filling

Melt the butter in a saucepan.

Stir in the flour and sugar.

Beat the egg yolk and milk together.

Add the egg mixture to the saucepan.

Stir constantly.

Bring the mixture to the boil.

Remove from the heat.

Whisk for 1 minute.

Add the vanilla extract.

Mix well.

Allow the mixture to cool down.

To Assemble The Tartlets

Spoon the filling into the cold pastry shells.

Top with the canned fruit.

Brush with the heated apricot jam.

Leave to set.

Chocolate And Strawberry Tartlets

Ingredients For Pastry Shells

37,5 ml margarine

37,5 ml sugar

1 egg

375 ml flour

7 ml baking powder

2 ml salt

5 ml vanilla extract

Ingredients For Chocolate Mousse

150 g dark chocolate

12,5 ml brandy

10 g butter

1 egg (separated)

100 ml cream (whipped)

Ingredients For Filling

Fresh strawberries (cut in half)

Whipped cream for garnishing

Method

Cream the margarine and sugar together until light and creamy.

Add the egg and vanilla extract.

Mix well.

Sift the flour, baking powder and salt together.

Combine the margarine mixture and the flour mixture together.

Mix well.

Wrap the pastry in plastic and refrigerate for 30 minutes.

Press the pastry into greased patty pans.

Bake at 180 degrees C for 15 to 20 minutes.

Cool the pastry shells in the patty pans before removing them from the pan.

Combine the chocolate, brandy, butter and egg yolks together.

Allow the mixture to cool.

Whisk the egg whites until stiff.

Gently fold the egg whites into the chocolate mixture together with the cream.

Spoon the chocolate mousse into the pastry shells (fill them halfway).

Arrange the strawberries on top on the chocolate mousse.

Garnish with whipped cream.

Macaron Recipes

Rose Petal Pistachio Macarons

Ingredients For Macarons

462,5 ml icing sugar

170 ml finely ground almonds

167,5 ml finely ground pistachio nuts

4 large egg whites

62,5 m granulated sugar

3 ml rose water

Few drops pink food coloring

Ingredients For Filling

62,5 ml shortening

62,5 ml butter

500 ml icing sugar

12,5 ml milk

5 ml rose water

Few drops pink food coloring

62,5 ml dried rose petals (crushed)

To Decorate

Candied rose petals

Method For Making Macarons

Sift the icing sugar, pistachio nuts and almonds together.

Whisk the egg whites with an electric beater on a medium speed until very soft peaks form. This should take about 1 to 2 minutes.

Add a 1/4 of the granulated sugar and whisk for another 45 seconds.

Repeat this process 3 more times.

Add a few drops of food coloring and the rose water.

Fold in 1/2 of the icing sugar, pistachio and almond mixture using a spatula. Fold in thoroughly.

Fold in the remaining mixture until just combined.

Be careful not to over mix.

Line the baking sheets with parchment paper.

Use a piping bag fitted with a 1/2 inch round tip to pipe the egg white mixture onto the baking sheets.

Pour the egg white mixture into the piping bag.

Pipe rounds about 1 inch in diameter and 1/2 inch thick onto the baking sheets.

When the baking sheet is full tap the baking sheet against the counter a few times to flatten the rounds and pop any air bubbles.

Allow the macarons to rest until they are no longer tacky to the touch. It should take about 30 minutes.

Heat the oven to 325 degrees F.

Position the oven racks in the top and bottom thirds of the oven.

Once the macarons are no longer tacky reduce the oven temperature to 300 degrees F.

Place the baking sheets in the oven and bake for 8 minutes and then rotate and swap the baking sheet positions.

Continue to bake until the macarons are very pale golden. It should take about 15 to 20 minutes.

Remove the baking sheets from the oven and allow the macarons to cool.

Method For Making Filling

Cream shortening and butter until light and fluffy.

Gradually add the icing sugar, one cup at a time.

Blend well on medium speed.

Add the milk, food coloring and rose water and beat until light and fluffy.

Mix in the crushed rose petals.

Assemble The Macarons

Make a small opening on the flat side of one macaron shell.

Place about a teaspoon of the filling over the opening.

Cover with another shell and twist until filling is evenly spread. Decorate the macarons with the candied rose petals.

Refrigerate macarons overnight before serving.

White Chocolate Ganache With Amaretto Macarons

Ingredients For Macarons

462,5 ml icing sugar

337,5 ml finely ground almonds

4 large egg whites

62,5 m granulated sugar

5 ml Amaretto

Ingredients For Filling

250 g white chocolate

187 ml cream

25 ml Amaretto

Method For Making Macarons

Sift the icing sugar and almonds together.

Whisk the egg whites with an electric beater on a medium speed until very soft peaks form. This should take about 1 to 2 minutes.

Add a 1/4 of the granulated sugar and whisk for another 45 seconds.

Repeat this process 3 more times.

Add the Amaretto.

Fold in 1/2 of the icing sugar and almond mixture using a spatula. Fold in thoroughly.

Fold in the remaining mixture until just combined.

Be careful not to over mix.

Line the baking sheets with parchment paper.

Use a piping bag fitted with a 1/2 inch round tip to pipe the egg white mixture onto the baking sheets.

Pour the egg white mixture into the piping bag.

Pipe rounds about 1 inch in diameter and 1/2 inch thick onto the baking sheets.

When the baking sheet is full tap the baking sheet against the counter a few times to flatten the rounds and pop any air bubbles.

Allow the macarons to rest until they are no longer tacky to the touch. It should take about 30 minutes.

Heat the oven to 325 degrees F.

Position the oven racks in the top and bottom thirds of the oven.

Once the macarons are no longer tacky reduce the oven temperature to 300 degrees F.

Place the baking sheets in the oven and bake for 8 minutes and then rotate and swap the baking sheet positions.

Continue to bake until the macarons are very pale golden. It should take about 15 to 20 minutes.

Remove the baking sheets from the oven and allow the macarons to cool.

Method For Making Filling

Melt the chocolate and cream over hot water.

Blend well.

Add the Amaretto.

Set aside to cool slightly.

Assemble The Macarons

Make a small opening on the flat side of one macaron shell.

Place about a teaspoon of the filling over the opening.

Cover with another shell and twist until filling is evenly spread.

Refrigerate macarons overnight before serving.

Meringue Recipes

Chocolate Meringue Kisses

Ingredients

4 egg whites

5 ml vanilla extract

2 ml cream of tartar

250 ml sugar

37,5 ml cocoa powder

White chocolate (melted)

Method

Whisk the egg whites until foamy.

Add the vanilla extract and the cream of tartar.

Whisk the egg whites until the meringue starts to look creamy and forms soft peaks. Add the sugar and the cocoa powder a little at a time.

Pour the meringue into a piping bag with a rosette nozzle.

Pipe rosettes of meringue on a parchment covered baking sheet. Bake at 225 degrees F for 1 hour.

Turn the oven off and open the oven door a crack.

Allow the meringues to cool for 5 to 10 minutes.

Remove from the oven and allow the meringues to cool.

Remove from parchment paper when cool.

Drizzle the melted chocolate over the meringues.

Chocolate Meringues

Ingredients

3 egg whites

90 g castor sugar

90 g icing sugar

30 g cocoa powder

150 ml cream (whipped)

3 chocolate flakes (broken into pieces)

Glace cherries (cut into pieces)

Method

Whisk the egg whites really stiff.

Add the castor sugar and continue whisking until the mixture is stiff again.

Add the sifted icing sugar and cocoa powder.

The mixture will become dry but it will mix in.

Pour the mixture into a piping bag with a rosette nozzle.

Pipe rosettes onto a greased baking sheet.

Bake 130 degrees C for 4 to five hours.

Sandwich the meringues together using the whipped cream.

Place the sandwiched meringues into paper candy cases.

Decorate the meringues with the flake and cherries.

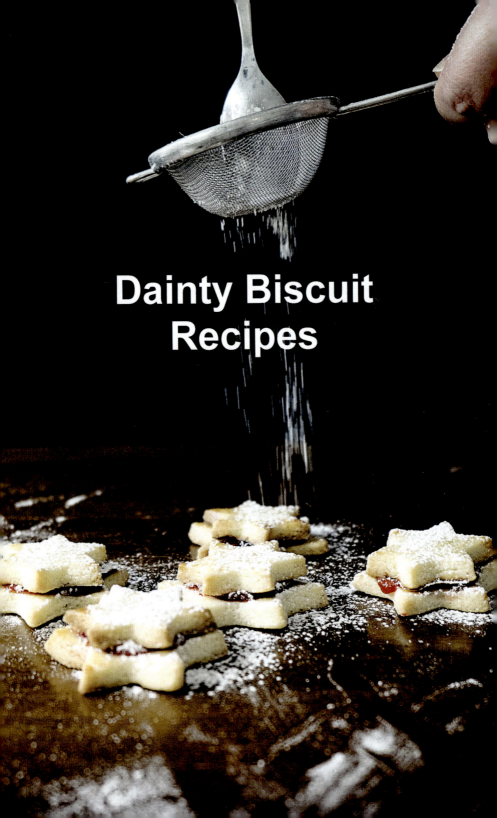

Dainty Biscuit
Recipes

Orange Brandy Cream Biscuit

Ingredients

- 125 g butter
- 37,5 ml sugar
- 1 egg yolk
- 5 ml orange zest
- 330 ml flour
- 125 g butter
- 80 ml icing sugar
- 3 ml vanilla extract
- 166 ml apricot jam
- 10 ml brandy
- Icing sugar

Method

Cream the butter and sugar.

Beat in eggs and orange zest.

Add flour.

Wrap cookie dough in cling wrap and chill for 1 hour.

Knead on lightly floured surface.

Roll the dough to a 3mm thickness.

Cut out rounds in the dough with a small cookie cutter. Take half of these rounds and cut out the centre.

Place on a greased baking sheet.

Bake for 12 to 15 minutes at 160 degrees C.

Allow cookies to cool.

Beat butter (125g), icing sugar and vanilla extract together.

Place filling into a piping bag and pipe a circle of filling around the edge of the cookies (rounds with no cut out).

Mix the brandy with the jam.

Spoon a bit of jam into the centre of the cookie and place cookie top (round with a cut out).

Viennese Biscuits

Ingredients

240 g margarine

90 g icing sugar

Zest of 1 orange

210 g flour

60 g corn flour

125 g chocolate (melted)

Icing sugar (sifted)

Chocolate Orange Liqueur Frosting

25 ml cocoa powder

25 ml orange liqueur

12,5 ml margarine

300 ml icing sugar

5 ml orange zest

Method

Cream the margarine and sugar together.

Add flour, orange zest and corn flour.

Mix to a fairly stiff consistency.

Place in a piping bag and pipe rosettes onto a greased baking sheet.

Bake for 10 to 15 minutes at 190 degrees C.

Allow cookies to cool.

To make the Chocolate Orange Liqueur Frosting, Blend the cocoa powder and the orange liqueur until smooth.

Beat in the margarine.

Continue beating with an electric beater until the mixture is light and fluffy.

Add the icing sugar and orange zest.

Mix well.

Sandwich 2 cookies together with Chocolate Orange Liqueur Frosting.

Dip the ends of the biscuits into the melted chocolate and then sprinkle with icing sugar.

Puff Pastry Recipes

Nougat Cream Puff Pastry

Ingredients

300 g pastry

50 g apricot jam (heated)

100 g icing sugar

12,5 ml lemon juice

12,5 ml lemon zest

450 g canned pitted cherries (drained but reserve the syrup)

50 g sugar

1 ml ground cinnamon

45 ml corn flour

125 ml cream

200 g nougat

12,5 ml Van Der Hum liqueur

30 ml gelatin

10 ml water

500 ml cream

Candies cherries for decoration

Method

Roll the pastry into a 200 X 500 mm rectangle.

Cut the pastry into 2 equal pieces.

Place the 2 pastry pieces onto a greased baking sheet.

Place the baking sheet in the freezer for 10 minutes.

Pre-heat the over to 225 degrees C.

Place the baking sheet into the oven and lower the heat immediately to 200 degrees C.

Bake for 10 to 12 minutes.

Spread the heated apricot jam over the pastry as soon as it is removed from the oven.

Combine the icing sugar, lemon juice and lemon zest together.

Spread the icing mixture over the apricot jam.

Cut each strip of pastry into 6 equal pieces.

Combine the cherry syrup, sugar and cinnamon together in a saucepan.

Boil until the syrup has halved in volume.

Mix the corn flour with a little water to form a paste.

Add the corn flour paste to the cherry syrup and boil until the syrup has thickened and is clear.

Stir constantly.

Remove the mixture from the heat.

Add the cherries to the syrup mixture.

Allow the mixture to cool down.

Slowly heat the cream in a double boiler.

Add the nougat.

Stir until the nougat has melted.

Add the Van Der Hum liqueur.

Sprinkle the gelatin over the water.

Allow the gelatine to become spongy.

Stir the spongy gelatine mixture into the nougat mixture.

Combine the nougat mixture and the cherry mixture together.

Mix well.

Beat the cream.

Fold the cream into the mixture.

Pack six of the pastry pieces against each other in a bread pan or make a "pan" out of aluminium foil.

Pour the filling over the pastry.

Pack the other 6 pastry pieces on top of the filling.

Refrigerate to allow the pastry to set.

Remove the pastry from the bread pan and cut each pastry piece into smaller pieces.

Decorate the slices with candied cherries.

Custard Puff Pastries

Ingredients

2 rolls of puff pastry

250 ml cream (beaten stiff)

200 ml cold milk

1 instant vanilla pudding mix

Icing sugar

Water

Candied flowers to decorate

Method

Defrost the pastry.

Cut the pastry into small squares.

Place the pastry squares onto a greased baking sheet.

Bake at 200 degrees C till golden brown.

Remove from the oven and allow the pastry squares to cool.

Combine the milk and instant vanilla pudding together.

Blend well.

Fold in the cream.

Refrigerate the custard filling for 5 minutes.

Spoon the custard filling between 2 pieces of puff pastry.

Mix a little icing sugar and hot water together to form a glace icing – it must be thick.

Drizzle the glace icing on the top of the pastry.

Decorate with candied flowers.

Made in United States
Orlando, FL
21 February 2025

58751785R00036